Kindergarten

Reading Comprehension Workbook

50 Stories
5 Questions per Story
Answer Keys Included

Volume 1
Created by Have Fun Teaching

Table of Contents

Name_____

My Pet Cat

Story By: Andrew Frinkle

Tom has a pet.

His pet is a cat.

His cat is orange and white.

His cat has a name.

Its name is Flash.

Flash is a boy cat.

Flash has four legs.

Flash has a long tail.

Flash can run fast.

Flash can climb trees.

Flash can catch mice.

Tom feeds his cat.

Flash eats many foods.

Flash eats dry cat food.

Flash eats canned cat food.

Flash drinks milk.

Tom loves his cat.

Name_____

My Pet Cat

Story By: Andrew Frinkle

Use the information in the story to answer the questions below.

1. FILL IN THE BLANK: His pet is a _____.
   A. Cow
   B. Horse
   C. Cat
   D. Dog

2. FILL IN THE BLANK: Flash has a long _____.
   A. Face
   B. Legs
   C. Ears
   D. Tail

3. FILL IN THE BLANK: Its name is _____.
   A. Cinnamon
   B. Whitey
   C. Mr. Whiskers
   D. Flash

4. YES OR NO: Does Flash eat canned cat food?
   A. Yes
   B. No

5. YES OR NO: Does Flash drink milk?
   A. Yes
   B. No

Name_____

My Pet Dog

Story By: Andrew Frinkle

Pam has a pet.

Her pet is a dog.

Her dog is brown and white.

Her dog has a name.

Its name is Peaches.

Peaches is a girl dog.

Peaches has four legs.

Peaches is furry.

Peaches has soft hair.

Peaches loves to run.

Pam feeds her dog.

Peaches eats dog food.

Peaches eats biscuits.

Peaches chews bones.

Peaches drinks water.

Pam loves her dog.

Name_____

My Pet Dog

Story By: Andrew Frinkle

Use the information in the story to answer the questions below.

1. FILL IN THE BLANK: Her pet is a _____.
   A. Cow
   B. Horse
   C. Cat
   D. Dog

2. FILL IN THE BLANK: Her dog is brown and _____.
   A. White
   B. Gray
   C. Brown
   D. Black

3. FILL IN THE BLANK: Peaches loves to _____.
   A. Eat
   B. Bark
   C. Sleep
   D. Run

4. YES OR NO: Does Peaches chew bones?
   A. Yes
   B. No

5. YES OR NO: Does Peaches eat biscuits?
   A. Yes
   B. No

Name_____

My Pet Fish

Story By: Andrew Frinkle

Susan has a pet.
Her pet is a fish.
Her fish is red and white.
Her fish has a name.
Its name is Goldie.

Goldie is a goldfish.
Goldie has no legs!
Goldie has fins.
Goldie has scales.
Goldie has big round eyes.
Goldie loves to swim.

Susan feeds her fish.
Goldie eats flake fish food.
Goldie eats fish pellets.
Goldie needs fresh water.

Susan loves her fish.

Name_____

My Pet Fish

Story By: Andrew Frinkle

Use the information in the story to answer the questions below.

1. FILL IN THE BLANK: Her pet is a _____.
    A. Fish
    B. Horse
    C. Cat
    D. Dog

2. FILL IN THE BLANK: Her fish is red and _____.
    A. White
    B. Gray
    C. Brown
    D. Black

3. FILL IN THE BLANK: Goldie loves to _____.
    A. Eat
    B. Swim
    C. Sleep
    D. Run

4. YES OR NO: Does Goldie need dirty water?
    A. Yes
    B. No

5. YES OR NO: Does Goldie eat cookies?
    A. Yes
    B. No

Name_____

My Pet Hamster

Story By: Andrew Frinkle

Hannah has a pet.
Her pet is a hamster.
Her hamster is brown.
Her hamster has a name.
Its name is Muffins.

Muffins is a girl hamster.
Muffins has four short legs.
Muffins has a short tail.
Muffins can run in a wheel.
Muffins can play in a tunnel.

Hannah feeds her hamster.
Muffins eats dry food.
Muffins eats veggies.
Muffins eats fruit.
Muffins eats nuts.
Muffins drinks water.

Hannah loves her hamster.

Name_____

My Pet Hamster

Story By: Andrew Frinkle

Use the information in the story to answer the questions below.

1. FILL IN THE BLANK: Her pet is a _____.
   - A. Rat
   - B. Mouse
   - C. Hamster
   - D. Guinea Pig

2. FILL IN THE BLANK: Muffins has four _____ legs.
   - A. Long
   - B. Skinny
   - C. Short
   - D. Cute

3. FILL IN THE BLANK: Its name is _____.
   - A. Muffins
   - B. Cupcake
   - C. Candy
   - D. Fluffy

4. YES OR NO: Does Muffins eat cookies?
   - A. Yes
   - B. No

5. YES OR NO: Does Muffins drink water?
   - A. Yes
   - B. No

Name_____

My Pet Horse

Story By: Andrew Frinkle

John has a pet.

His pet is a horse.

His horse is brown.

His horse has a name.

Its name is Dusty.

Dusty is a boy horse.

Dusty has four legs.

Dusty is tall.

Dusty has a tail.

His tail is long.

John feeds his horse.

Dusty eats many foods.

Dusty eats apples.

Dusty eats carrots.

Dusty eats hay.

John loves his horse.

Name_____

My Pet Horse

Story By: Andrew Frinkle

Use the information in the story to answer the questions below.

1. FILL IN THE BLANK: His pet is a _____.
   A. Cow
   B. Horse
   C. Cat
   D. Dog

2. FILL IN THE BLANK: Dusty has _____ legs.
   A. One
   B. Two
   C. Three
   D. Four

3. FILL IN THE BLANK: His horse is _____.
   A. White
   B. Gray
   C. Brown
   D. Black

4. YES OR NO: Does Dusty eat apples?
   A. Yes
   B. No

5. YES OR NO: Does Dusty eat pie?
   A. Yes
   B. No

Name_____

My Pet Lizard

Story By: Andrew Frinkle

James has a pet.

His pet is a lizard.

His lizard is green.

His lizard has a name.

Its name is Green Bean.

Green Bean is a boy iguana.

Green Bean has four legs.

Green Bean has scales.

Green Bean has a tail.

His tail is really, really long.

James feeds his lizard.

Green Bean eats greens.

Green Bean eats fruits.

Green Bean eats veggies.

Green Bean does NOT eat meat or bugs.

James loves his lizard.

My Pet Lizard

Story By: Andrew Frinkle

Use the information in the story to answer the questions below.

1. FILL IN THE BLANK: His pet is a _____.
   A. Snake
   B. Frog
   C. Turtle
   D. Lizard

2. FILL IN THE BLANK: Green Bean has _____ legs.
   A. One
   B. Two
   C. Three
   D. Four

3. FILL IN THE BLANK: His lizard is _____.
   A. Blue
   B. Purple
   C. Green
   D. Orange

4. YES OR NO: Does Green Bean eat meat?
   A. Yes
   B. No

5. YES OR NO: Does Green Bean have a long tail?
   A. Yes
   B. No

Name_____

My Pet Pig

Story By: Andrew Frinkle

Peter has a pet.

His pet is a pig.

His pig is pink.

His pig has a name.

Its name is Porky.

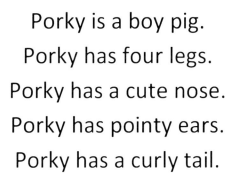

Porky is a boy pig.

Porky has four legs.

Porky has a cute nose.

Porky has pointy ears.

Porky has a curly tail.

Peter feeds his pig.

Porky eats many foods.

Porky eats veggies.

Porky eats grass.

Porky eats bugs.

Porky eats leftovers!

Peter loves his pig.

My Pet Pig

Story By: Andrew Frinkle

Use the information in the story to answer the questions below.

1. FILL IN THE BLANK: His pet is a _____.
   A. Pig
   B. Horse
   C. Goat
   D. Cow

2. FILL IN THE BLANK: Porky has a _____ tail.
   A. Long
   B. Short
   C. Round
   D. Curly

3. FILL IN THE BLANK: His pig is _____.
   A. Yellow
   B. White
   C. Pink
   D. Gray

4. YES OR NO: Does Porky eat grass?
   A. Yes
   B. No

5. YES OR NO: Does Porky have a cute nose?
   A. Yes
   B. No

Name_____

My Pet Rabbit

Story By: Andrew Frinkle

Sara has a pet.

Her pet is a rabbit.

Her rabbit is tan and white.

Her rabbit has a name.

Its name is Jumpy.

Jumpy is a girl rabbit.

Jumpy has four legs.

Jumpy has a short white tail.

Jumpy has long ears.

Jumpy has very soft fur.

Jumpy likes to jump!

Sara feeds her rabbit.

Jumpy eats rabbit food.

Jumpy eats veggies.

Jumpy eats grass.

Jumpy does NOT eat meat.

Jumpy drinks water.

Sara loves her rabbit.

Name_____

My Pet Rabbit

Story By: Andrew Frinkle

Use the information in the story to answer the questions below.

1. FILL IN THE BLANK: Her pet is a _____.
   A. Rat
   B. Rabbit
   C. Cat
   D. Dog

2. FILL IN THE BLANK: Jumpy has long _____.
   A. Teeth
   B. Legs
   C. Ears
   D. Tail

3. FILL IN THE BLANK: Jumpy likes to _____.
   A. Bounce
   B. Sing
   C. Eat
   D. Jump

4. YES OR NO: Does Jumpy eat meat?
   A. Yes
   B. No

5. YES OR NO: Does Jumpy eat veggies?
   A. Yes
   B. No

Name_____

My Pet Snake

Story By: Andrew Frinkle

Tara has a pet.

Her pet is a snake.

Her snake is green.

Her snake has a name.

Its name is Scales.

Scales is a boy snake.

His skin is scaly.

He does not have fur.

He does not have feathers.

Scales has no legs!

Scales has a long tail.

Scales can slither fast!

Scales likes warm places.

Tara feeds her snake.

Scales eats bugs.

Scales eats mice.

Scales eats living food.

Scales drinks water.

Tara loves her snake.

Name_____

My Pet Snake

Story By: Andrew Frinkle

Use the information in the story to answer the questions below.

1. FILL IN THE BLANK: Her pet is a _____.
   A. Lizard
   B. Turtle
   C. Snake
   D. Frog

2. FILL IN THE BLANK: Scales has _____ legs!
   A. No
   B. Two
   C. Four
   D. Eight

3. FILL IN THE BLANK: Its name is _____.
   A. Greenie
   B. Slither
   C. Hisssss
   D. Scales

4. YES OR NO: Does Scales have fur?
   A. Yes
   B. No

5. YES OR NO: Does Scales drink tea?
   A. Yes
   B. No

Name_____

The Weather is Cloudy

Story By: Andrew Frinkle

How is the weather today?
The weather is cloudy.

The sky is blue.
The sky is white.
There are lots of clouds.

The clouds cover the sun.
They move across the sky.
They are fluffy.
They are white.

Some clouds are high.
Some clouds are low.
Some clouds are big.
Some clouds are small.

How is the weather today?
The weather is cloudy.

Name_____

The Weather is Cloudy

Story By: Andrew Frinkle

Use the information in the story to answer the questions below.

1. FILL IN THE BLANK: The _____ is white.
   A. Car
   B. House
   C. Cat
   D. Sky

2. Which of these does NOT describe clouds?
   A. Big
   B. Small
   C. Ugly
   D. High

3. FILL IN THE BLANK: Some _____ are high.
   A. Cars
   B. Clouds
   C. Rain
   D. Coats

4. YES OR NO: Is the weather rainy?
   A. Yes
   B. No

5. YES OR NO: Is the weather cloudy?
   A. Yes
   B. No

Name_____

The Weather is Cold

Story By: Andrew Frinkle

How is the weather today?
The weather is cold.

It is not warm.
It is not hot.
It is COLD!
I can see my breath.

I need a hat.
I need mittens.
I need a coat.
I need boots.

Try to stay warm.
Sit by the fire.
Stay inside.
Have hot chocolate.

How is the weather today?
The weather is cold.

Name_____

The Weather is Cold

Story By: Andrew Frinkle

Use the information in the story to answer the questions below.

1. FILL IN THE BLANK: The weather is _____.
   A. Cold
   B. Cool
   C. Warm
   D. Hot

2. What is one way to stay warm?
   A. Do NOT wear a coat.
   B. Take a cold shower.
   C. Take a nap.
   D. Have hot chocolate.

3. FILL IN THE BLANK: Sit by the _____.
   A. TV
   B. Fire
   C. Oven
   D. Door

4. YES OR NO: Does the person in the story need a swimsuit?
   A. Yes
   B. No

5. YES OR NO: Does the person in the story need a hat?
   A. Yes
   B. No

Name_____

The Weather is Dry

Story By: Andrew Frinkle

How is the weather today?
The weather is dry.

It is warm.
It is dry.
There is no rain.

The grass is brown.
The ground is dusty.
The leaves are yellow.

Plants need rain.
It is too dry!
It is like a desert.
I hope it rains soon.

How is the weather today?
The weather is dry.

Name_____

The Weather is Dry

Story By: Andrew Frinkle

Use the information in the story to answer the questions below.

1. FILL IN THE BLANK: The weather is _____.
   A. Hot
   B. Cold
   C. Wet
   D. Dry

2. What color is the grass?
   A. Yellow
   B. Green
   C. Brown
   D. Pink

3. What color are the leaves?
   A. Yellow
   B. Green
   C. Brown
   D. Pink

4. FILL IN THE BLANK: It is like a _____.
   A. Desert
   B. Forest
   C. Ocean
   D. Sea

5. YES OR NO: Do the plants need rain?
   A. Yes
   B. No

Name_____

The Weather is Foggy

Story By: Andrew Frinkle

How is the weather today?
The weather is foggy.

It is hard to see.
It is gray outside.
There is fog.

It is a cloud.
It is all around.
I can not see far.

Here is the sun.
The fog is going.
Now I can see.

How is the weather today?
The weather is foggy.

Name_____

The Weather is Foggy

Story By: Andrew Frinkle

Use the information in the story to answer the questions below.

1. FILL IN THE BLANK: The weather is _____.
   A. Cloudy
   B. Foggy
   C. Sunny
   D. Windy

2. What color is the fog?
   A. White
   B. Black
   C. Gray
   D. Purple

3. FILL IN THE BLANK: I can not _____ far.
   A. See
   B. Walk
   C. Swim
   D. Run

4. YES OR NO: Is the fog all around?
   A. Yes
   B. No

5. YES OR NO: Does the sun make the fog go away?
   A. Yes
   B. No

Name_____

The Weather is Hot

Story By: Andrew Frinkle

How is the weather today?
The weather is hot.

The sun is hot.
The air is warm.
Stay in the shade.

It is hot.
It is sweaty.
It is not cool!

Have a cold drink.
Eat some ice cream.
Take a swim.
Use a fan.
Stay cool.

How is the weather today?
The weather is hot.

Name_____

The Weather is Hot

Story By: Andrew Frinkle

Use the information in the story to answer the questions below.

1. FILL IN THE BLANK: The weather is _____.
   A. Cold
   B. Cool
   C. Warm
   D. Hot

2. What is one way to stay cool?
   A. Eat some ice cream.
   B. Go running.
   C. Take a nap.
   D. Eat some hot dogs.

3. FILL IN THE BLANK: Take a _____.
   A. Nap
   B. Seat
   C. Swim
   D. Book

4. YES OR NO: Is it sweaty?
   A. Yes
   B. No

5. YES OR NO: Is it cold?
   A. Yes
   B. No

The Weather is Rainy

Story By: Andrew Frinkle

How is the weather today?
The weather is rainy.

The sky is gray.
It is not blue.
Where did the sun go?
I do not see it.

The clouds are dark.
The rain falls down.
The rain hits the windows.
The grass is wet.

I wear a raincoat.
I use an umbrella.
I feel the cold rain.
I step over puddles.

How is the weather today?
The weather is rainy.

Name_____

The Weather is Rainy

Story By: Andrew Frinkle

Use the information in the story to answer the questions below.

1. FILL IN THE BLANK: The sky is _____.
   A. White
   B. Gray
   C. Blue
   D. Orange

2. YES OR NO: Is the rain cold?
   A. Yes
   B. No

3. FILL IN THE BLANK: The grass is _____.
   A. Green
   B. Wet
   C. Rain
   D. Soft

4. YES OR NO: Does the person in the story use an umbrella?
   A. Yes
   B. No

5. YES OR NO: Is the weather sunny?
   A. Yes
   B. No

Name_____

The Weather is Snowy

Story By: Andrew Frinkle

How is the weather today?
The weather is snowy.

The air is cold.
The sky is grey.
It is winter.
It is snowing.

White flakes fall.
They are soft.
They are small.
They are cold.

I wear a hat.
I wear gloves.
I wear a coat.
I wear boots.

How is the weather today?
The weather is snowy.

Name_____

The Weather is Snowy

Story By: Andrew Frinkle

Use the information in the story to answer the questions below.

1. FILL IN THE BLANK: White _____ fall.
   A. Snow
   B. Flakes
   C. Stuff
   D. Rain

2. YES OR NO: Is the air cold?
   A. Yes
   B. No

3. FILL IN THE BLANK: I _____ a hat.
   A. Have
   B. Buy
   C. Take
   D. Wear

4. Which of these does the person NOT wear?
   A. Hat
   B. Gloves
   C. Swimsuit
   D. Boots

5. YES OR NO: Is the weather stormy?
   A. Yes
   B. No

Name_____

The Weather is Stormy

Story By: Andrew Frinkle

How is the weather today?
The weather is stormy.

The wind is fast.
It is strong.

The sky is dark.
There are many clouds.

Lightning flashes.
Thunder cracks.
Rain falls.
Wind blows.

This is a big storm.

How is the weather today?
The weather is stormy.

Name_____

The Weather is Stormy

Story By: Andrew Frinkle

Use the information in the story to answer the questions below.

1. FILL IN THE BLANK: The weather is _____.
   A. Sunny
   B. Super
   C. Stormy
   D. Snowy

2. Which of these is NOT happening?
   A. Rain falls.
   B. Lightning Flashes.
   C. Thunder Cracks.
   D. Snow falls.

3. FILL IN THE BLANK: This is a _____ storm.
   A. Happy
   B. Big
   C. Small
   D. Nice

4. YES OR NO: Is the sky blue?
   A. Yes
   B. No

5. YES OR NO: Is the wind fast?
   A. Yes
   B. No

Name_____

The Weather is Sunny

Story By: Andrew Frinkle

How is the weather today?

The weather is sunny.

The sky is clear.

It is so blue!

There are no clouds.

The sun is bright.

The sun is warm.

It feels good!

The plants are growing.

The beach is full.

What a nice day.

How is the weather today?

The weather is sunny.

Name_____

The Weather is Sunny

Story By: Andrew Frinkle

Use the information in the story to answer the questions below.

1. FILL IN THE BLANK: The weather is _____.
   A. Cloudy
   B. Sunny
   C. Stormy
   D. Windy

2. YES OR NO: Are there any clouds?
   A. Yes
   B. No

3. FILL IN THE BLANK: The sky is _____.
   A. Clean
   B. Clear
   C. Cloudy
   D. Candy

4. YES OR NO: Is it a bad day?
   A. Yes
   B. No

5. YES OR NO: Does the sun feel good?
   A. Yes
   B. No

The Weather is Sunny

Story By: Andrew Frinkle

Use the information in the story to answer the questions below.

Name_____

The Weather is Windy

Story By: Andrew Frinkle

How is the weather today?
The weather is windy.

The wind is fast.
The wind is strong.
The wind is slow.
The wind is gentle.

Leaves blow.
Flags flap.
Kites fly.
Boats sail.

On a hot day,
the wind is cool.
On a cold day,
the wind is freezing!

How is the weather today?
The weather is windy.

The Weather is Windy

Story By: Andrew Frinkle

Use the information in the story to answer the questions below.

1. FILL IN THE BLANK: The weather is _____.
   A. Cloudy
   B. White
   C. Silly
   D. Windy

2. What word was NOT used to describe the wind?
   A. Fast
   B. Slow
   C. Strong
   D. Pretty

3. FILL IN THE BLANK: Boats _____.
   A. Sail
   B. Fly
   C. Swim
   D. Eat

4. YES OR NO: On a hot day, is the wind cool?
   A. Yes
   B. No

5. YES OR NO: On a cold day, is the wind hot?
   A. Yes
   B. No

Name_____

Things that are Black

Story By: Andrew Frinkle

There are many colors.
I see **black**.
Many things are **black**.

I see…

Night skies are **black**.
Blackberries are **black**.
Coffee is **black**.
Cats are **black**.
Birds are **black**.
Dogs are **black**.
Ants are **black**.
Spiders are **black**.
Hair is **black**.
Charcoal is **black**.

Many things are **black**.
Can *you* see **black**?

Name_____

Things that are Black

Story By: Andrew Frinkle

Use the information in the story to answer the questions below.

1. FILL IN THE BLANK: I see _____.
   A. White
   B. Blue
   C. Brown
   D. Black

2. Which of these is NOT a black animal from the story?
   A. Cats
   B. Birds
   C. Dogs
   D. Elephants

3. FILL IN THE BLANK: Charcoal _____ black.
   A. Am
   B. Be
   C. Is
   D. Are

4. YES OR NO: Is coffee black?
   A. Yes
   B. No

5. YES OR NO: Are blueberries black?
   A. Yes
   B. No

Name_____

Things that are Blue

Story By: Andrew Frinkle

There are many colors.
I see blue.
Many things are blue.

I see...

The sky is blue.
Water is blue.
Cars are blue.
Flowers are blue.
Birds are blue.
Shoes are blue.
Clothes are blue.
Blueberries are blue.
Paint is blue.
Crayons are blue.

Many things are blue.
Can *you* see blue?

© HaveFunTeaching.com

Name_____

Things that are Blue

Story By: Andrew Frinkle

Use the information in the story to answer the questions below.

1. FILL IN THE BLANK: I see _____.
   A. White
   B. Yellow
   C. Blue
   D. Green

2. Which of these is NOT something blue from the story?
   A. Shoes
   B. Crayons
   C. Socks
   D. Cars

3. FILL IN THE BLANK: Birds _____ blue.
   A. Am
   B. Be
   C. Is
   D. Are

4. YES OR NO: Are blueberries blue?
   A. Yes
   B. No

5. YES OR NO: Are monkeys blue?
   A. Yes
   B. No

Name_____

Things that are Brown

Story By: Andrew Frinkle

There are many colors.
I see **brown**.
Many things are **brown**.

I see...

Potatoes are **brown**.
Dirt is **brown**.
Paper bags are **brown**.
Tree trunks are **brown**.
Wood is **brown**.
Turkeys are **brown**.
Bears are **brown**.
Deer are **brown**.
Horses are **brown**.
Seeds are **brown**.

Many things are **brown**.
Can *you* see **brown**?

Name_____

Things that are Brown

Story By: Andrew Frinkle

Use the information in the story to answer the questions below.

1. FILL IN THE BLANK: I see _____.
   A. Yellow
   B. Brown
   C. White
   D. Black

2. Which of these is NOT a brown animal from the story?
   A. Deer
   B. Turkeys
   C. Bears
   D. Elephants

3. FILL IN THE BLANK: Wood _____ brown.
   A. Am
   B. Be
   C. Is
   D. Are

4. YES OR NO: Are paper bags brown?
   A. Yes
   B. No

5. YES OR NO: Are potatoes brown?
   A. Yes
   B. No

Name_____

Things that are Green

Story By: Andrew Frinkle

There are many colors.
I see green.
Many things are green.

I see…

Trees are green.
Grass is green.
Leaves are green.
Clovers are green.
Limes are green.
Melons are green.
Cars are green.
Books are green.
Paint is green.
Snakes are green.

Many things are green.
Can *you* see green?

Name_____

Things that are Green

Story By: Andrew Frinkle

Use the information in the story to answer the questions below.

1. FILL IN THE BLANK: I see _____.
   A. White
   B. Yellow
   C. Blue
   D. Green

2. Which of these is NOT something green from the story?
   A. Apples
   B. Trees
   C. Grass
   D. Leaves

3. FILL IN THE BLANK: Paint _____ green.
   A. Am
   B. Be
   C. Is
   D. Are

4. YES OR NO: Are limes green?
   A. Yes
   B. No

5. YES OR NO: Are clouds green?
   A. Yes
   B. No

Name_____

Things that are Orange

Story By: Andrew Frinkle

There are many colors.
I see orange.
Many things are orange.

I see…

Oranges are orange.
The sun is orange.
Butterflies are orange.
Pumpkins are orange.
Carrots are orange.
Leaves are orange.
Tigers are orange.
Cats are orange.
Flowers are orange.
Crayons are orange.

Many things are orange.
Can *you* see orange?

Things that are Orange

Story By: Andrew Frinkle

Use the information in the story to answer the questions below.

1. FILL IN THE BLANK: I see _____.
   A. Orange
   B. Yellow
   C. Red
   D. Pink

2. Which of these is NOT an orange food from the story?
   A. Oranges
   B. Carrots
   C. Tigers
   D. Pumpkins

3. FILL IN THE BLANK: The sun _____ orange.
   A. Am
   B. Be
   C. Is
   D. Are

4. YES OR NO: Are oranges orange?
   A. Yes
   B. No

5. YES OR NO: Is grass orange?
   A. Yes
   B. No

Name_____

Things that are Purple

Story By: Andrew Frinkle

There are many colors.
I see **purple**.
Many things are **purple**.

I see…

Violets are **purple**.
Eggplant is **purple**.
Sunsets are **purple**.
Petunias are **purple**.
Grapes are **purple**.
Bruises are **purple**.
Lavender is **purple**.
Dresses are **purple**.
Paint is **purple**.
Crayons are **purple**.

Many things are **purple**.
Can *you* see **purple**?

Things that are Purple

Story By: Andrew Frinkle

Use the information in the story to answer the questions below.

1. FILL IN THE BLANK: I see _____.
   A. Red
   B. Purple
   C. Blue
   D. Black

2. Which of these is NOT something purple from the story?
   A. Violets
   B. Eggplant
   C. Grapes
   D. Cookies

3. FILL IN THE BLANK: Violets _____ purple.
   A. Am
   B. Be
   C. Is
   D. Are

4. YES OR NO: Is the sun purple?
   A. Yes
   B. No

5. YES OR NO: Are grapes purple?
   A. Yes
   B. No

Name_____

Things that are Red

Story By: Andrew Frinkle

There are many colors.
I see red.
Many things are red.

I see...

Roses are red.
Apples are red.
Watermelon is red.
Fire trucks are red.
Cherries are red.
Strawberries are red.
Cars are red.
Birds are red.
Stop signs are red.
Tomatoes are red.

Many things are red.
Can *you* see red?

Name_____

Things that are Red

Story By: Andrew Frinkle

Use the information in the story to answer the questions below.

1. FILL IN THE BLANK: I see _____.
   A. Orange
   B. Yellow
   C. Red
   D. Purple

2. Which of these is NOT something red from the story?
   A. Apples
   B. Trees
   C. Roses
   D. Birds

3. FILL IN THE BLANK: Cherries _____ red.
   A. Am
   B. Be
   C. Is
   D. Are

4. YES OR NO: Are oranges red?
   A. Yes
   B. No

5. YES OR NO: Are fire trucks red?
   A. Yes
   B. No

Name_____

Things that are White

Story By: Andrew Frinkle

There are many colors.
I see **white**.
Many things are **white**.

I see…

Clouds are **white**.
Ice is **white**.
Snow is **white**.
Horses are **white**.
Rabbits are **white**.
Marshmallows are **white**.
Bread is **white**.
Chickens are **white**.
Flowers are **white**.
Dresses are **white**.

Many things are **white**.
Can *you* see **white**?

Name_____

Things that are White

Story By: Andrew Frinkle

Use the information in the story to answer the questions below.

1. FILL IN THE BLANK: I see _____.
   A. White
   B. Blue
   C. Brown
   D. Black

2. Which of these is NOT a white animal from the story?
   A. Monkeys
   B. Horses
   C. Chickens
   D. Rabbits

3. FILL IN THE BLANK: Bread _____ white.
   A. Am
   B. Be
   C. Is
   D. Are

4. YES OR NO: Is the sky white?
   A. Yes
   B. No

5. YES OR NO: Are lemons white?
   A. Yes
   B. No

Name_____

Things that are Yellow

Story By: Andrew Frinkle

There are many colors.
I see yellow.
Many things are yellow.

I see…

Bananas are yellow.
Corn is yellow.
Cheese is yellow.
Flowers are yellow.
Butterflies are yellow.
Lemons are yellow.
Lions are yellow.
Pineapple is yellow.
Chicks are yellow.
School Buses are yellow.

Many things are yellow.
Can *you* see yellow?

Name_____

Things that are Yellow

Story By: Andrew Frinkle

Use the information in the story to answer the questions below.

1. FILL IN THE BLANK: I see _____.
    A. Orange
    B. Yellow
    C. Red
    D. Pink

2. Which of these is NOT a yellow animal from the story?
    A. Lions
    B. Butterflies
    C. Chicks
    D. Flowers

3. FILL IN THE BLANK: Cheese _____ yellow.
    A. Am
    B. Be
    C. Is
    D. Are

4. YES OR NO: Is corn yellow?
    A. Yes
    B. No

5. YES OR NO: Are school buses yellow?
    A. Yes
    B. No

Name_____

Things that come in 1's

Story By: Andrew Frinkle

Some things come in **1's**.
There is only **one** of them.
Can you think of any?

You have **1** head.
You have **1** nose.
You have **1** mouth.
You have **1** body.

We have **one** sun.
We have **one** moon.

A year has **1** Christmas.
A year has **1** Easter.
A year has **1** Halloween.

Many things come in **1's**.
There is only **one** of them.
Can _you_ think of more?

Name_____

Things that come in 1's

Story By: Andrew Frinkle

Use the information in the story to answer the questions below.

1. FILL IN THE BLANK: Some things come in _____.
    A. 1's
    B. 2's
    C. 3's
    D. 4's

2. Which of these is NOT something you only have 1 of?
    A. Head
    B. Mouth
    C. Eyes
    D. Nose

3. FILL IN THE BLANK: A year has 1 _____ .
    A. Day
    B. Christmas
    C. Sunday
    D. Week

4. YES OR NO: Do we have one sun?
    A. Yes
    B. No

5. YES OR NO: Do we have two moons?
    A. Yes
    B. No

Name_____

Things that come in 2's

Story By: Andrew Frinkle

Some things come in **2's**.
There are **two** of them.
Can you think of any?

You have **2** ears.
You have **2** eyes.
You have **2** hands.
You have **2** feet.
You have **2** arms.
You have **2** legs.

Twins are **two** people.
Two things is a **pair**.
A **couple** is **two** people.
A **duo** is **two** things.

Many things come in **2's**.
There are **two** of them.
Can _you_ think of more?

Things that come in 2's

Story By: Andrew Frinkle

Use the information in the story to answer the questions below.

1. FILL IN THE BLANK: Some things come in _____.
   A. 1's
   B. 2's
   C. 3's
   D. 4's

2. Which of these is NOT something you have 2 of?
   A. Feet
   B. Mouth
   C. Ears
   D. Eyes

3. FILL IN THE BLANK: _____ are two people.
   A. Brothers
   B. Sisters
   C. Twins
   D. Triplets

4. YES OR NO: Are two things a pair?
   A. Yes
   B. No

5. YES OR NO: Is a couple two people?
   A. Yes
   B. No

Name_____

Things that come in 3's

Story By: Andrew Frinkle

A few things come in **3's**.
There are **three** of them.
Can you think of any?

A clock has **3** hands.
A season is **3** months.
A tricycle has **3** wheels.
A clover has **3** leaves.
A stool has **3** legs.
A tripod has **3** legs.
A triangle has **3** sides.

Triplets are **three** people.
A **trio** is **three** things.

Many things come in **3's**.
There are **three** of them.
Can *you* think of more?

Name_____

Things that come in 3's

Story By: Andrew Frinkle

Use the information in the story to answer the questions below.

1. FILL IN THE BLANK: A few things come in _____.
   A. 1's
   B. 2's
   C. 3's
   D. 4's

2. Which of these has 3 legs?
   A. A dog
   B. A boy
   C. A stool
   D. A clock

3. FILL IN THE BLANK: A clock has 3 _____.
   A. Hands
   B. Feet
   C. Legs
   D. Arms

4. YES OR NO: Are three things a pair?
   A. Yes
   B. No

5. YES OR NO: Are triplets three people?
   A. Yes
   B. No

Name_____

Things that come in 4's

Story By: Andrew Frinkle

A lot of things come in **4's**.
There are **four** of them.
Can you think of any?

Many things have **4** legs!
A dog has **4** legs.
A cat has **4** legs.
So do cows, goats, horses, tigers, bears, lions, elephants...
WHEW!

A year has **4** seasons.
A car has **4** wheels.
A <u>lucky</u> clover has **4** leaves.
A chair has **4** legs.
A rectangle has **4** sides.
A square has **4** sides.

Quadruplets are **four** people.
A **quartet** is **four** things.

Many things come in **4's**.
There are **four** of them.
Can *you* think of more?

Name_____

Things that come in 4's

Story By: Andrew Frinkle

Use the information in the story to answer the questions below.

1. FILL IN THE BLANK: A lot of things come in _____.
    A. 1's
    B. 2's
    C. 3's
    D. 4's

2. Which of these does NOT have 4 legs?
    A. A dog
    B. A cat
    C. A fish
    D. A goat

3. FILL IN THE BLANK: A year has 4 _____.
    A. Days
    B. Weeks
    C. Months
    D. Seasons

4. YES OR NO: Does a square have 4 sides?
    A. Yes
    B. No

5. YES OR NO: Does a car have 4 wheels?
    A. Yes
    B. No

Name_____

Things that come in 5's

Story By: Andrew Frinkle

Some things come in **5's**.
There are **five** of them.
Can you think of any?

Pentagons have **5** sides.
There are **$5** bills.
Nickels are **5** cents.
Clock numbers are **5** minutes each.
A spare tire is a **5**th car wheel.
There are **5** oceans.
You might be **5** years old.
You have **5** fingers.
You have **5** toes.

Quintuplets are **five** people.
A **quintet** is **five** things.

Some things come in **5's**.
There are **five** of them.
Can _you_ think of more?

Things that come in 5's

Story By: Andrew Frinkle

Use the information in the story to answer the questions below.

1. FILL IN THE BLANK: Some things come in _____.
   A. 5's
   B. 6's
   C. 7's
   D. 8's

2. Which of these shapes has 5 sides?
   A. A triangle
   B. A pentagon
   C. A square
   D. A circle

3. FILL IN THE BLANK: There are 5 _____.
   A. Seas
   B. Lakes
   C. Rivers
   D. Oceans

4. YES OR NO: Is a quintet 5 things?
   A. Yes
   B. No

5. YES OR NO: Is a nickel 6 cents?
   A. Yes
   B. No

Name_____

Things that come in 6's

Story By: Andrew Frinkle

A few things come in **6's**.

There are **six** of them.

Can you think of any?

Hexagons have **6** sides.

Bolts and Nuts have **6** sides.

6 is half a dozen.

6 months is half a year.

Bugs have **6** legs.

There are **6** players on a hockey team.

You might be **6** years old.

Is your dad **6** feet tall?

A few things come in **6's**.

There are **six** of them.

Can _you_ think of more?

Name_____

Things that come in 6's

Story By: Andrew Frinkle

Use the information in the story to answer the questions below.

1. FILL IN THE BLANK: A few things come in _____.
   A. 5's
   B. 6's
   C. 7's
   D. 8's

2. Which of these shapes has 6 sides?
   A. An octagon
   B. A pentagon
   C. A hexagon
   D. A decagon

3. FILL IN THE BLANK: 6 is half a _____.
   A. Dozen
   B. Set
   C. Team
   D. Pack

4. YES OR NO: Are there 5 players on a hockey team?
   A. Yes
   B. No

5. YES OR NO: Do bugs have 6 legs?
   A. Yes
   B. No

Name_____

Things that come in 7's

Story By: Andrew Frinkle

A few things come in **7's**.
There are **seven** of them.
Can you think of any?

Heptagons have **7** sides.
Weeks have **7** days.
7 is a lucky number!
You might be **7** years old.
There are **7** continents.
Sevens is a card game.
Baseball has a **7**th inning stretch.
July is the **7**th month.
There are **7** wonders of the world.

A few things come in **7's**.
There are **seven** of them.
Can *you* think of more?

Name_____

Things that come in 7's

Story By: Andrew Frinkle

Use the information in the story to answer the questions below.

1. FILL IN THE BLANK: A few things come in _____.
   A. 5's
   B. 6's
   C. 7's
   D. 8's

2. How many days are in a week?
   A. 5
   B. 6
   C. 7
   D. 8

3. FILL IN THE BLANK: 7 is a _____ number.
   A. Silly
   B. Cool
   C. Fun
   D. Lucky

4. YES OR NO: Is June the 7th month?
   A. Yes
   B. No

5. YES OR NO: Does basketball have the 7th inning stretch?
   A. Yes
   B. No

Name_____

Things that come in 8's

Story By: Andrew Frinkle

A few things come in **8's**.
There are **eight** of them.
Can you think of any?

Octagons have **8** sides.
Spiders have **8** legs.
An octopus has **8** legs.
Stop signs have **8** sides.
Crazy **Eights** is a card game.
August is the **8**th month.
8 hot dogs come in a pack.
8 buns come in a pack, too.
There are **8** pints in a gallon.
8 crayons come in a box.

A few things come in **8's**.
There are **eight** of them.
Can _you_ think of more?

Name_____

Things that come in 8's

Story By: Andrew Frinkle

Use the information in the story to answer the questions below.

1. FILL IN THE BLANK: A few things come in _____.
   A. 5's
   B. 6's
   C. 7's
   D. 8's

2. What is the 8th month?
   A. February
   B. August
   C. October
   D. September

3. FILL IN THE BLANK: _____ Eights is a card game.
   A. Silly
   B. Crazy
   C. Funny
   D. Lucky

4. YES OR NO: Does a stop sign have 8 sides?
   A. Yes
   B. No

5. YES OR NO: Do spiders have 10 legs?
   A. Yes
   B. No

Things that come in 9's

Story By: Andrew Frinkle

Very few things come in **9's**.
There are **nine** of them.
Can you think of any?

September is the **9**th month.
Baseball has **9** innings.
A baseball team has **9** players.
Tic-Tac-Toe has **9** squares.
Nine Ball is a pool game.
Golf is **9** holes.
Is **9** o'clock your bedtime?
Cats have **9** lives.
Nines is a card game.

Very few things come in **9's**.
There are **nine** of them.
Can *you* think of more?

Name_____

Things that come in 9's

Story By: Andrew Frinkle

Use the information in the story to answer the questions below.

1. FILL IN THE BLANK: Very few things come in _____.
   A. 7's
   B. 8's
   C. 9's
   D. 10's

2. What is the 9th month?
   A. February
   B. August
   C. October
   D. September

3. FILL IN THE BLANK: Nines is a _____ game.
   A. Dice
   B. Card
   C. Board
   D. Video

4. YES OR NO: Does Tic-Tac-Toe have 9 squares?
   A. Yes
   B. No

5. YES OR NO: Does baseball have 9 innings?
   A. Yes
   B. No

Name_____

Things that come in 10's

Story By: Andrew Frinkle

Lots of things come in **10**'s.
There are **tens** of them.
Can you think of any?

October is the **10**th month.
Do you have a **$10** bill?
Dimes are **10** cents.
A decade is **10** years.
Crabs have **10** legs.
Squids have **10** limbs.
Shrimp have **10** legs.
Bowling has **10** pins.
You have **10** fingers.
You have **10** toes.
Decagons have **10** sides.

Lots of things come in **10**'s.
There are **tens** of them.
Can _you_ think of more?

Things that come in 10's

Story By: Andrew Frinkle

Use the information in the story to answer the questions below.

1. FILL IN THE BLANK: Lots of things come in _____.

   A. 7's

   B. 8's

   C. 9's

   D. 10's

2. What is the 10th month?

   A. February

   B. August

   C. October

   D. September

3. Which of these animals does NOT have 10 legs?

   A. Crabs

   B. Squids

   C. Spiders

   D. Shrimp

4. YES OR NO: Are dimes 10 cents?

   A. Yes

   B. No

5. YES OR NO: Is a decade 12 years?

   A. Yes

   B. No

Name_____

How Many is That?

Story By: Andrew Frinkle

I have one dog.
How many is that?

I have two red hats.
How many is that?

I have three books.
How many is that?

I have four toy robots.
How many is that?

I have five fingers on my hand.
How many is that?

I have six good friends.
How many is that?

That's a lot!
Do you know more numbers?

How Many is That?

Story By: Andrew Frinkle

Use the information in the story to answer the questions below.

1. How many dogs are there?
    A. 1
    B. 2
    C. 3
    D. 4

2. How many books are there?
    A. 1
    B. 2
    C. 3
    D. 4

3. How many robots are there?
    A. 1
    B. 2
    C. 3
    D. 4

4. How many fingers are there?
    A. 3
    B. 4
    C. 5
    D. 6

5. How many friends are there?
    A. 3
    B. 4
    C. 5
    D. 6

Name_____

What Animal is That?

Story By: Andrew Frinkle

FOLD THE PICTURES OVER TO HIDE THE ANSWERS

It has a long tail. It has whiskers. It says meow.

What animal is that?

It is a cat.

It has scales. It swims. It lives in water.

What animal is that?

It is a fish.

It has long hair. It has a long tail. It barks.

What animal is that?

It is a dog.

It has a curly tail. It is fat. It says oink, oink.

What animal is that?

It is a pig.

It is big. It has spots. It says moo.

What animal is that?

It is a cow.

It climbs trees. It eats bananas. It says hoo hoo hoo.

What animal is that?

It is a monkey.

Name_____

What Animal is That?

Story By: Andrew Frinkle

Use the information in the story to answer the questions below.

1. Which animal says meow?

   A. dog

   B. cat

   C. fish

   D. monkey

2. Which animal eats bananas?

   A. dog

   B. cat

   C. fish

   D. monkey

3. Which animal lives in water?

   A. dog

   B. cat

   C. fish

   D. monkey

4. Which animal barks?

   A. dog

   B. cat

   C. fish

   D. monkey

5. Which animal was not in the story?

   A. cow

   B. horse

   C. monkey

   D. dog

Name_____

What Color is This?
Story By: Andrew Frinkle

What color is the sky now?

The sky is red

The sky is orange

It is sunrise.

What color is the sky now?

The sky is blue

The clouds are white.

It is day time.

What color is the sky now?

The sky is grey.

The lightning is yellow.

It is stormy.

What color is the sky now?

The sky is purple.

The sky is pink.

It is sunset.

What color is the sky now?

The sky is black.

The stars are bright.

It is night time.

Good night!

Name_____

What Color is This?

Story By: Andrew Frinkle

Use the information in the story to answer the questions below.

1. What colors is the sky at sunrise?
    A. red and orange
    B. blue and white
    C. grey and yellow
    D. purple and pink

2. What colors is the sky in day time?
    A. red and orange
    B. blue and white
    C. grey and yellow
    D. purple and pink

3. What colors is the sky when it is stormy?
    A. red and orange
    B. blue and white
    C. grey and yellow
    D. purple and pink

4. What colors is the sky at sunset?
    A. red and orange
    B. blue and white
    C. grey and yellow
    D. purple and pink

5. Which color is NOT mentioned in the story?
    A. yellow
    B. brown
    C. blue
    D. black

Name_____

What Day is This?

Story By: Andrew Frinkle

It is the first day of the week.

What day is this?

It is Sunday. You do not go to school.

It is the second day of the week.

What day is this?

It is Monday. You go to school.

It is the third day of the week.

What day is this?

It is Tuesday. You go to school.

It is the fourth day of the week.

What day is this?

It is Wednesday. You go to school.

It is the fifth day of the week.

What day is this?

It is Thursday. You go to school.

It is the sixth day of the week.

What day is this?

It is Friday. School is done!

It is the seventh day of the week.

What day is this?

It is Saturday. Have some fun!

Now we go back to Sunday...

Name_____

What Day is This?

Story By: Andrew Frinkle

Use the information in the story to answer the questions below.

1. What is the first day (day 1)?
   A. Sunday
   B. Monday
   C. Wednesday
   D. Friday

2. What is the fourth day (day 4)?
   A. Sunday
   B. Monday
   C. Wednesday
   D. Friday

3. What is the second day (day 2)?
   A. Sunday
   B. Monday
   C. Wednesday
   D. Friday

4. What day is school done?
   A. Sunday
   B. Monday
   C. Wednesday
   D. Friday

5. What day is for having fun?
   A. Thursday
   B. Friday
   C. Saturday
   D. Sunday

Name_____

What Flavor is This?

Story By: Andrew Frinkle

What flavor is this?
The apple is red.
It is crunchy.
The flavor is **SWEET!**

What flavor is this?
The pepper is green.
It is hot!
The flavor is **SPICY!**

What flavor is this?
The lemon is yellow.
It smells fresh.
The flavor is **SOUR!**

What flavor is this?
The chips are tan.
They are greasy.
The flavor is **SALTY!**

What flavor is this?
The peanuts have shells.
They are chewy.
The flavor is **NUTTY!**

What flavor is this?
The berries are purple.
They are juicy.
The flavor is **TART!**

Name_____

What Flavor is This?

Story By: Andrew Frinkle

Use the information in the story to answer the questions below.

1. What flavor is the apple?
   A. sweet
   B. spicy
   C. salty
   D. tart

2. What flavor is the pepper?
   A. sweet
   B. spicy
   C. salty
   D. tart

3. What flavor are the berries?
   A. sweet
   B. spicy
   C. salty
   D. tart

4. What flavor are the chips?
   A. sweet
   B. spicy
   C. salty
   D. tart

5. Which flavor is NOT mentioned in the story?
   A. tart
   B. bitter
   C. sweet
   D. nutty

Name_____

What Food is This?

Story By: Andrew Frinkle

It has long noodles. It has red sauce on top.
What food is this?
It is <u>spaghetti</u>!

It has bread. It has meat. It has vegetables.
What food is this?
It is a <u>sandwich</u>!

It has broth. It has meat. It has vegetables.
What food is this?
It is <u>soup</u>!

It has curly noodles. It has cheese.
What food is this?
It is <u>mac n' cheese</u>!

It has a soft inside. It has frosting outside.
What food is this?
It is <u>cake</u>!

It has crust. It has cheese. It has toppings.
What food is this?
It is <u>pizza</u>!

It has meat inside. It is crunchy outside.
What food is this?
It is <u>fried chicken</u>!

Name_____

What Food is This?

Story By: Andrew Frinkle

Use the information in the story to answer the questions below.

1. Which food has long noodles?
   A. spaghetti
   B. mac n' cheese
   C. cake
   D. pizza

2. Which food has curly noodles?
   A. spaghetti
   B. mac n' cheese
   C. cake
   D. pizza

3. Which food has frosting on the outside?
   A. pie
   B. cake
   C. ice cream
   D. pizza

4. Which food has a crust?
   A. fried chicken
   B. spaghetti
   C. cake
   D. pizza

5. Which food is NOT mentioned in the story?
   A. soup
   B. cookies
   C. fried chicken
   D. sandwich

What Game is That?

Story By: Andrew Frinkle

It has X's and O's. Get 3 in a row!
What game is that?
It is **Tic-Tac-Toe**.

You kick a ball into a net.
What game is that?
It is **soccer**.

You clap your hands.
What game is that?
It is **patty-cake**.

You hit a ball with a bat.
What game is that?
It is **baseball.**

You hide from a friend. You find a friend.
What game is that?
It is **hide and seek**.

You jump over a rope.
What game is that?
It is **jump rope**.

You have to chase a friend. You have to catch them.
What game is that?
It is **tag**.

Name_____

What Game is That?

Story By: Andrew Frinkle

Use the information in the story to answer the questions below.

1. What game has X's and O's?
   A. Tic-Tac-Toe
   B. Soccer
   C. Patty-Cake
   D. Baseball

2. What game has clapping?
   A. Tic-Tac-Toe
   B. Soccer
   C. Patty-Cake
   D. Baseball

3. What game has a bat and ball?
   A. Tic-Tac-Toe
   B. Soccer
   C. Patty-Cake
   D. Baseball

4. Which game has jumping?
   A. Hide and Seek
   B. Jump Rope
   C. Tag
   D. Soccer

5. Which game has hiding?
   A. Hide and Seek
   B. Jump Rope
   C. Tag
   D. Soccer

What Kind of Weather is That?

Story By: Andrew Frinkle

The sky is blue. The sun is hot. There are no clouds.
What kind of weather is that?
It's **sunny.**

The sky is blue. There are lots of clouds.
What kind of weather is that?
It's **cloudy.**

The sky is grey. It is windy. Water is falling.
What kind of weather is that?
It's **rainy.**

The sky is dark. There is lightning. There is rain.
What kind of weather is that?
It's **stormy.**

The sky is cloudy. Small, cold flakes are falling.
What kind of weather is that?
It's **snowy.**

The air is moving fast. My hair is blowing.
What kind of weather is that?
It's **windy.**

Name_____

What Kind of Weather is That?

Story By: Andrew Frinkle

Use the information in the story to answer the questions below.

1. MATCHING: The sky is blue. The sun is hot. There are no clouds.
   A. windy
   B. stormy
   C. sunny
   D. snowy

2. MATCHING: The sky is dark. There is lightning. There is rain.
   A. windy
   B. stormy
   C. sunny
   D. snowy

3. MATCHING: The air is moving fast. My hair is blowing.
   A. windy
   B. stormy
   C. sunny
   D. snowy

4. MATCHING: The sky is cloudy. Small, cold flakes are falling.
   A. windy
   B. stormy
   C. sunny
   D. snowy

5. Which flavor is NOT a kind of weather from the story?
   A. rainy
   B. cloudy
   C. stormy
   D. bad

Name_____

What Shape is That?

Story By: Andrew Frinkle

It is round. It has no corners.

What shape is that?

It is a **circle**.

It is almost round. It looks like an egg.

What shape is that?

It is an **oval**.

It has three sides. It has three corners.

What shape is that?

It is a **triangle**.

It has four sides. They are all the same.

What shape is that?

It is a **square**.

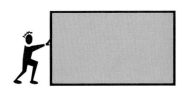

It has four sides. Two are longer.

What shape is that?

It is a **rectangle**.

It has five sides. It has five corners.

What shape is that?

It is a **pentagon**.

Name_____

What Shape is That?

Story By: Andrew Frinkle

Use the information in the story to answer the questions below.

1. Which two shapes are mostly round?
   A. circle and square
   B. circle and oval
   C. triangle and pentagon
   D. square and rectangle

2. Which two shapes have four sides?
   A. circle and square
   B. circle and oval
   C. triangle and pentagon
   D. square and rectangle

3. Which shape has 3 sides?
   A. square
   B. rectangle
   C. triangle
   D. pentagon

4. Which shape has 5 sides?
   A. square
   B. rectangle
   C. triangle
   D. pentagon

5. Which of these is NOT mentioned in the story?
   A. octagon
   B. pentagon
   C. rectangle
   D. oval

Name_____

What Time is This?

Story By: Andrew Frinkle

It is time to get up. It is morning. Brush your teeth.
What time is this?
It's 7 o'clock.

It is time to eat. It is breakfast time. Eat up!
What time is this?
It's 8 o'clock.

It is time to eat lunch. Are you hungry?
What time is this?
It's 12 o'clock.

It is time to take a nap. Are you sleepy?
What time is this?
It's 2 o'clock.

It is time to eat dinner. What is for dinner, Mom?
What time is this?
It's 5 o'clock.

It is time to go to bed. It is night time.
What time is this?
It's 9 o'clock.

Name_____

What Time is This?

Story By: Andrew Frinkle

Use the information in the story to answer the questions below.

1. What time is it to wake up?
   A. 7 o'clock
   B. 8 o'clock
   C. 12 o'clock
   D. 2 o'clock

2. What time is it to eat lunch?
   A. 7 o'clock
   B. 8 o'clock
   C. 12 o'clock
   D. 2 o'clock

3. What time is it to take a nap?
   A. 7 o'clock
   B. 8 o'clock
   C. 12 o'clock
   D. 2 o'clock

4. What time is it to eat dinner?
   A. 4 o'clock
   B. 5 o'clock
   C. 6 o'clock
   D. 7 o'clock

5. What time is it to go to bed?
   A. 7 o'clock
   B. 8 o'clock
   C. 9 o'clock
   D. 10 o'clock

Name_____

Which Way is That?

Story By: Andrew Frinkle

My name is John. I am five years old. I know my directions.

I see clouds above.
Which way is that?
It is **up**.

I see a hole in the ground.
Which way is that?
It is **down**.

I eat with this hand.
Which way is that?
It is **right**.

I have another hand, too.
Which way is that?
It is **left.**

I look ahead.
Which way is that?
It is to the **front**.

I look behind me.
Which way is that?
It is to the **back**.

Name_____

Which Way is That?

Story By: Andrew Frinkle

Use the information in the story to answer the questions below.

1. Which way are the clouds?
   A. up
   B. down
   C. left
   D. right

2. Which way is the hole in the ground?
   A. up
   B. down
   C. left
   D. right

3. Which hand does John eat with?
   A. up
   B. down
   C. left
   D. right

4. Which way is looking ahead?
   A. left
   B. front
   C. back
   D. up

5. Which way is looking behind?
   A. left
   B. front
   C. back
   D. up

Name_____

Who is That?

Story By: Andrew Frinkle

This person is a girl.
She cooks and cleans.
She has two kids.
She is married to DAD.
Who is that?
It's **MOM**!

This person is a boy.
He works and helps out.
He has two kids.
He is married to MOM.
Who is that?
It's **DAD**!

This person is a boy.
He plays with SISTER.
He is younger than her.
He is only four.
Who is that?
It's **SON**!

This person is a girl.
She helps MOM.
She is older than her BROTHER.
She is only six.
Who is that?
It's **DAUGHTER**!

Name_____

Who is That?

Story By: Andrew Frinkle

Use the information in the story to answer the questions below.

1. How many girls are in the family?

    A. 0

    B. 1

    C. 2

    D. 3

2. How many boys are in the family?

    A. 0

    B. 1

    C. 2

    D. 3

3. How many people are in the family?

    A. 1

    B. 2

    C. 3

    D. 4

4. Who is the youngest?

    A. mom

    B. dad

    C. sister

    D. brother

5. Which of these is NOT mentioned in the story?

    A. pets

    B. mom

    C. sister

    D. dad

Kindergarten

K

Answer Key

Kindergarten

MY PET CAT	PAGE 5
1.C	
2.D	
3.D	
4.A	
5.A	

MY PET LIZARD	PAGE 15
1.D	
2.D	
3.C	
4.B	
5.A	

MY PET DOG	PAGE 7
1.D	
2.A	
3.D	
4.A	
5.A	

MY PET PIG	PAGE 17
1.A	
2.D	
3.C	
4.A	
5.A	

MY PET FISH	PAGE 9
1.A	
2.A	
3.B	
4.B	
5.B	

MY PET RABBIT	PAGE 19
1.B	
2.C	
3.D	
4.B	
5.A	

MY PET HAMSTER	PAGE 11
1.C	
2.C	
3.A	
4.B	
5.A	

MY PET SNAKE	PAGE 21
1.C	
2.A	
3.D	
4.B	
5.B	

MY PET HORSE	PAGE 13
1.B	
2.D	
3.C	
4.A	
5.B	

THE WEATHER IS CLOUDY	PAGE 23
1.D	
2.C	
3.B	
4.B	
5.A	

Kindergarten K

THE WEATHER IS COLD　　PAGE 25
1.A
2.D
3.B
4.B
5.A

THE WEATHER IS SNOWY　　PAGE 35
1.B
2.A
3.B
4.C
5.B

THE WEATHER IS DRY　　PAGE 27
1.D
2.C
3.A
4.A
5.A

THE WEATHER IS STORMY　　PAGE 37
1.C
2.D
3.B
4.B
5.A

THE WEATHER IS FOGGY　　PAGE 29
1.B
2.C
3.A
4.A
5.A

THE WEATHER IS SUNNY　　PAGE 39
1.B
2.B
3.B
4.B
5.A

THE WEATHER IS HOT　　PAGE 31
1.D
2.A
3.C
4.A
5.B

THE WEATHER IS WINDY　　PAGE 41
1.D
2.D
3.A
4.A
5.B

THE WEATHER IS RAINY　　PAGE 33
1.B
2.A
3.B
4.A
5.B

THINGS THAT ARE BLACK　　PAGE 43
1.D
2.D
3.C
4.A
5.B

Kindergarten

THINGS THAT ARE BLUE — PAGE 45
1. C
2. C
3. D
4. A
5. B

THINGS THAT ARE RED — PAGE 55
1. C
2. B
3. D
4. B
5. A

THINGS THAT ARE BROWN — PAGE 47
1. B
2. D
3. C
4. A
5. A

THINGS THAT ARE WHITE — PAGE 57
1. A
2. A
3. C
4. B
5. B

THINGS THAT ARE GREEN — PAGE 49
1. D
2. A
3. C
4. A
5. B

THINGS THAT ARE YELLOW — PAGE 59
1. B
2. D
3. C
4. A
5. A

THINGS THAT ARE ORANGE — PAGE 51
1. A
2. C
3. C
4. A
5. B

THINGS THAT COME IN 1'S — PAGE 61
1. A
2. C
3. B
4. A
5. B

THINGS THAT ARE PURPLE — PAGE 53
1. B
2. D
3. D
4. B
5. A

THINGS THAT COME IN 2'S — PAGE 63
1. B
2. B
3. C
4. A
5. A

Have Fun Teaching

Reading Comprehension Workbook

Kindergarten

K

Have Fun Teaching   Reading Comprehension Workbook

Kindergarten

K

WHAT COLOR IS THAT?   PAGE 85
1.A
2.B
3.C
4.D
5.B

WHAT KIND OF WEATHER IS THAT? P. 95
1.C
2.B
3.A
4.D
5.D

WHAT DAY IS THIS?   PAGE 87
1.A
2.C
3.B
4.D
5.C

WHAT SHAPE IS THAT?   PAGE 97
1.B
2.D
3.C
4.D
5.A

WHAT FLAVOR IS THIS?   PAGE 89
1.A
2.B
3.D
4.C
5.B

WHAT TIME IS THIS?   PAGE 99
1.A
2.C
3.D
4.B
5.C

WHAT FOOD IS THIS?   PAGE 91
1.A
2.B
3.B
4.D
5.B

WHICH WAY IS THAT?   PAGE 101
1.A
2.C
3.D
4.B
5.C

WHAT GAME IS THAT?   PAGE 93
1.A
2.C
3.D
4.B
5.A

WHO IS THAT?   PAGE 103
1.C
2.C
3.D
4.D
5.A

Made in United States
North Haven, CT
26 September 2023

42000114R00062